MASTERING THE CLOCK

A Comprehensive Guide to Time Management

By

DAWSON ROBERT

BOOK DESCRIPTION

"Mastering the Clock: A Comprehensive Guide to Time Management" is your ultimate guide to regaining control of your most valuable asset: time. In today's fast-paced environment, good time management is critical to success and well-being. This book provides a comprehensive arsenal of ideas, techniques, and concepts to help you manage your time, achieve your objectives, and live a more balanced and satisfying life.

"Mastering the Clock" addresses all aspects of efficient time management, including creating clear goals and priorities, fighting procrastination, controlling distractions, and practicing self-care. Each chapter includes practical insights, actionable guidance, and real-life examples to help you master the art of time management.

This book contains something for everyone, whether you're a busy professional, a student juggling several commitments, or someone who wants to take charge of their time. With its straightforward approach, "Mastering the Clock" teaches you to make the most of every hour, allowing you to accomplish more in less time and create a life that represents your goals and values.

By applying the principles stated in "Mastering the Clock" to your daily life, you will learn to increase productivity, reduce stress, and find better fulfilment in both your professional and personal endeavors. Whether you're looking for job advancement, personal development, or just a better work-life balance, this thorough guide will help you reach your greatest potential and live your best life.

DISCLAIMER

Copyright © Garner Hoffman. 2022. All rights reserved.
Before duplicating or reproducing this document, the publisher's permission must be obtained. As a result, the contents cannot be electronically stored, transferred, or saved in a database. The document cannot be copied, scanned, faxed, or retained without the publisher's or creator's permission.

Table of Contents

Introduction 5
Understanding Time Management 6
Assessing Your Current Time Usage 9
Setting Clear Goals and Priorities 12
Planning and Scheduling 15
Overcoming Procrastination 18
Optimizing Productivity 21
Managing Distractions 24
Delegating and Outsourcing 27
Strategies for Time Recovery 30
Maintaining Work-Life Balance 33
CONCLUSION 35

Introduction

Time is the most inaccessible yet most valuable resource we have. It is the great equalizer, constantly ticking away for all humanity, regardless of status or riches. Despite its universal nature, the way we perceive and use time differs substantially from person to person. Some people appear to simply glide through their days, doing things with ease while still finding time for leisure and relaxation. Others feel like they're constantly battling the clock, trying to keep up with their never-ending to-do list.

In today's fast-paced world, where technology has made information more accessible than ever before, our time has never been more valuable. We are inundated with emails, messages, and constant streams of content that compete for our attention. In the midst of this mayhem, efficient time management has become not only a luxury but a requirement for success.

"Mastering the Clock: A Comprehensive Guide to Time Management" is intended to be your road map to reclaiming control of your most valuable asset: time. Whether you're a busy professional, a student juggling several commitments, or someone who just wants to get the most out of each day, this guide will help you master the art of time management.

Understanding Time Management

Before going into the practical strategies and techniques for efficiently managing your time, it's critical to first define what time management implies. At its foundation, time management is the process of organizing and prioritizing tasks and activities in order to make the most of the limited time available. It's about being deliberate about how you spend your time, ensuring that you're focusing on activities that are consistent with your goals and values.

In today's world, where distractions abound and demands on our time are constantly increasing, mastering time management is more difficult than ever. It demands not only discipline and focus but also a thorough understanding of oneself and one's priorities. It is about making deliberate decisions about how you spend your time, rather than merely reacting to whatever comes your way.

Why Time Management Matters
The value of excellent time management cannot be overemphasized. It has an impact on all aspects of our lives, including our personal relationships and career achievements. Here are a few reasons why mastering time management is critical.
Increased productivity when you manage your time properly, you can get more done in less time. Prioritizing work and avoiding distractions allows you to focus your energy on the most important activities, resulting in higher productivity and better results.
Reduced stress one of the most common reasons for stress in modern life is feeling overwhelmed by the sheer quantity of chores and duties we have to manage. Effective time management reduces stress by bringing structure and clarity to our days. When you have a clear strategy in place, you can approach your chores with confidence, knowing that you have enough time to do everything that needs to be done.

Time management requires you to priorities and make choices about how you spend your time. By analyzing the importance and urgency of each activity, you gain a better understanding of what is genuinely important to you. This, in turn, improves your decision-making abilities as you become more competent at discerning between jobs that are critical and those that can be assigned or postponed.

Better work-life balance

In today's hyper-connected society, striking a healthy work-life balance can seem unattainable. However, efficient time management can assist you in striking the appropriate balance between your work and personal lives. Setting limits and prioritizing self-care can help you avoid burnout and make time for the activities that make you happy and fulfilled outside of work.

Common Challenges
Despite its numerous advantages, mastering time management is not without its hurdles. In fact, for many people, it may be a lifelong struggle. Here are some frequent issues that people confront while attempting to manage their time properly.

Procrastination
Procrastination is arguably the most significant impediment to successful time management. We've all been tempted to put off things until the last minute, whether because they're difficult or just because we'd rather do something more pleasurable. However, procrastination ultimately increases stress and decreases productivity.

Over commitment
In our eagerness to satisfy others or prove ourselves, many of us overcommit. We agree to every request, even if it means straining ourselves thinly and sacrificing our personal well-being. Learning to say no and create boundaries is critical for successful time management.

Distractions
In today's digital world, diversions abound. Whether it's the ping of a new email or the allure of social media, remaining focused on the task at hand can be a continual challenge. Learning to avoid distractions and stay focused is essential for good time management.

Lack of prioritization
Without defined priorities, it's easy to become overwhelmed by the sheer number of chores competing for your attention. Learning to prioritize tasks according to their relevance and urgency is critical for good time management. Otherwise, you risk squandering time on low-value tasks and ignoring those that are actually important.

Unrealistic expectations
Many of us have a tendency to underestimate the length of jobs or overestimate our ability to complete them in a given amount of time. This might lead to feelings of anger and disappointment when we fall short of our goals. Learning to set realistic objectives and manage your time effectively is critical for long-term success.

In the pages that follow, we'll go over real ideas and techniques for overcoming these frequent obstacles and mastering the art of time management. Setting clear goals and priorities, as well as using good planning and scheduling tactics, will teach you how to manage your time and achieve more success in all aspects of your life.

So, are you prepared to go on this adventure to master the clock? If so, let's dive in and learn how to maximize your productivity with smart time management.

Assessing Your Current Time Usage

To effectively manage your time, you must first understand how you are currently using it. This necessitates taking a step back and critically assessing your habits, routines, and behaviors. In this section, we'll look at different self-assessment approaches to assist you in obtaining insight into your present time management.

Self-Assessment Techniques

Self-assessment is the practice of reflecting on one's own behavior and actions to identify opportunities for development. When it comes to time management, self-assessment can be an effective method for learning about your habits and suggesting areas where you can improve. Here are some self-assessment tools that may help you evaluate your current time usage:

1. **Time tracking**: Begin by maintaining a careful record of your daily activities. This can be as basic as writing down your actions in a notebook or utilizing a time tracking tool to track your progress. Keep track of your professional and personal activities, including time spent on assignments, breaks, and leisure activities.

2. **Reflective Journals**: Set aside time each day to think about how you spent your time and how productive you felt. Consider the tasks you completed, the challenges you faced, and how you might improve your time management in the future. Writing in a reflection journal might help you recognize patterns and trends in your behavior over time.

3. **Self-Questioning**: Ask yourself questions about your time management practices, such as identifying your top time wasters.

Am I devoting enough time to projects that will help me achieve my goals?
Do I have a clear strategy for each day, or do I improvise?
How do I feel by the end of each day? Am I content with what I have accomplished?
What adjustments can I implement to improve my time management abilities? 4.

Peer Feedback: Sometimes we aren't the best judges of our own actions. Consider getting input from friends, family members, or coworkers on your time management skills. They may provide significant ideas and viewpoints that you had not considered.

By using these self-assessment approaches, you will obtain a better understanding of how you currently spend your time and where you may improve.

Identifying time wasters

After assessing your current time usage, identify any activities or behaviors that are taking up unnecessary time. These timewasters can take various forms, including obvious distractions like social media and more subtle habits like multitasking. Here are some frequent time-wasters to watch out for:

1. **Social Media and Internet Surfing**: It's no secret that social media and the internet can be huge time wasters. These technologies can be useful for remaining connected and informed, but they can also be extremely distracting. Set social media boundaries, and consider using website blockers or applications to help you stay focused.

2. **Multitasking**: Contrary to popular belief, multitasking is not the most effective approach to completing tasks. In reality, it can reduce productivity by diverting your focus and lowering the quality of your output. Instead, concentrate on one task at a time and give it your undivided attention before proceeding to the next.

3. **Poorly Defined Goals**: Without defined goals and priorities, it's easy to become bogged down by low-value tasks that don't help you get closer to your goals. Take the time to identify your goals and divide them into manageable steps. This will allow you to stay focused on what is genuinely important and avoid wasting time on activities that are not in line with your goals.

4. **Procrastination** is the enemy of good time management. Procrastination, whether it's putting off unpleasant jobs or waiting until the last minute to begin a project, just adds stress and reduces productivity. Identify the underlying causes of your procrastination and devise solutions to overcome them.

5. **Meetings and Interruptions**: While conferences and interruptions are frequently inevitable, they can also be significant time wasters if not handled properly. Set limitations for your availability, and consider scheduling uninterrupted work time on your calendar. Additionally, be strategic about which meetings you attend and decline ones that aren't necessary.

6. **Lack of planning**: Without a clear plan for how you'll spend your time, it's easy to get caught up in the day's commotion, leaving you feeling overwhelmed and unproductive. Plan your day or week ahead of time, allocating specific time for critical tasks and activities.

By identifying and correcting these frequent time wasters, you'll be better able to maximize your time and achieve your objectives.

Analyze your daily routine
Your daily routine has a huge impact on how you manage your time. Analyzing your routine allows you to identify areas for improvement and make changes that will increase your efficiency and productivity. Here are a few tips to help you analyze your everyday routine.

1. **Plan out your day**: Begin by outlining your regular daily schedule, from the moment you wake up until you go to bed. Include all activities, both work-related and personal, with as much detail as feasible.
2. **Identify patterns and trends**: Once you have a good understanding of your daily routine, look for patterns and trends in your behavior. Are there specific times of the day when you are most productive? Are there any activities that frequently take longer than expected? Identifying these patterns will enable you to optimize your routine for maximum efficiency.
3. **Evaluate Time Usage**: Take a hard look at how you spend your time each day. Are there any tasks that can be removed or delegated? Are there any ways to optimize your process or automate monotonous tasks? Look for strategies to improve your daily routine's efficiency and productivity.
4. **Establish priorities**: Based on your findings, determine the most critical tasks and activities in your daily routine. These are the activities that correspond to your goals and priorities and require the most time and attention. Make sure you schedule dedicated time for these high-priority projects.
5. **Experiment and iterate**: Your daily schedule is not set in stone. It is critical to be adaptable and open to experimenting with various ways to determine what works best for you. Make minor changes to your routine and assess the impact on your productivity and overall well-being. Iterate based on your results until you find a regimen that suits you.

By evaluating your current time usage, identifying time wasters, and analyzing your daily routine, you'll be well on your way to mastering the clock and attaining greater success in all aspects of your life.

Setting Clear Goals and Priorities

Goals provide the basis for efficient time management. They provide direction, focus, and motivation, allowing you to priorities work and manage your time effectively. In this section, we'll look at the value of goals in time management, the concepts of SMART goal setting, and numerous prioritization approaches to help you achieve your goals efficiently.

Goals are important in time management.

Goals are a road map for your life. They give you something to aspire for while also providing a sense of purpose and direction. Without clear goals, it's easy to become lost in the day-to-day grind, jumping from one duty to the next with no real sense of accomplishment.

Goals are important in time management: because they help you prioritize your tasks and allocate your time more effectively. Setting specific goals allows you to identify what is truly important to you and focus your attention on activities that will help you achieve your goals. This not only boosts your productivity, but it also provides you with a better sense of accomplishment and happiness as you work towards your goals.

Setting smart goals

Effective goal planning requires more than simply a vague sense of what you want to accomplish. It is about defining specified, measurable, attainable, relevant, and time-bound (SMART) goals with defined success criteria. The following is a breakdown of each component of SMART goal-setting:

1. **Specific**: Make your goals clear and specific, leaving no space for misunderstanding. Instead of expressing, "I want to lose weight," a more specific aim may be, "I want to lose 10 pounds in three months."

2. **Measurable**: Your objectives should be quantifiable so that you can monitor your progress and assess your success. This could include setting numerical targets or

milestones to aim for. For example, "I want to increase my monthly sales by 20%."
3. **Achievable**: Your objectives should be reasonable and feasible given your existing situation and resources. While it is necessary to push oneself, establishing unreasonable goals can result in dissatisfaction and burnout. Make sure your goals are attainable, but will require effort to achieve.
4. **Relevant**: Your goals should be related to your overall aims and in line with your beliefs and priorities. They should be beneficial to your long-term growth and success, rather than arbitrary or irrelevant.
5. **Time-bound**: Your goals should have a specific deadline or timeline for completion. This creates a sense of urgency and accountability, which motivates you to take action and progress towards your goals.
By adhering to the SMART criteria, you can ensure that your objectives are well-defined, attainable, and in line with your vision for success.

Prioritization Techniques

Once you've established clear goals, the next step is to priorities your tasks and activities to ensure that you're allocating your time and energy to the activities that will get you closer to your goals. Here are some prioritization tactics to help you manage your time more effectively:
1. **ABC method**: Priorities your chores into three groups: A (urgent and important), B (important but not urgent), and C (not urgent or important). Focus on finishing your A tasks first, then your B tasks, and ultimately your C duties.
2. **The Eisenhower Matrix**: Divide your duties into four quadrants according to their urgency and importance:
Quadrant 1: Urgent and Important Duties
Quadrant 2: Important but Not Urgent Tasks
Quadrant 3: Urgent but not critical jobs.
Quadrant 4: Jobs that are not urgent or significant.
Focus on finishing activities in Quadrant 1 first, then Quadrant 2, and so on.
3. **Time Blocking**: Set aside certain blocks of time in your schedule for various jobs and activities. This helps to avoid procrastination and guarantees that you devote focused time to your top objectives.
4. **The 80:20 Rule**: This concept, often known as the Pareto Principle, argues that 80% of your results are achieved with 20% of your effort. Identify and priorities the tasks and activities that will add the most value to your goals.
5. **Eat That Frog: Brian** Tracy popularized this strategy, which motivates you to do the most difficult or unpleasant chore first thing in the morning. Getting things out of the way early prepares you for the productive day ahead.
6. **Weighted Decision Matrix**: In more complex decision-making procedures, use a weighted decision matrix to assess the importance and influence of various

possibilities. Assign weights to each criterion based on its importance, and then use the matrix to compare and priorities your choices.

By using these prioritization approaches, you can ensure that you are allocating your time and energy to tasks that will bring you closer to your objectives and maximize your overall effectiveness.

Planning and Scheduling

Effective planning and scheduling are essential components of efficient time management. By proactively organizing your chores and activities, you can increase productivity, reduce stress, and ensure that you are making progress towards your goals. In this section, we'll look at different time-management strategies and techniques.

Effective planning strategies

Effective planning begins with a clear grasp of your objectives, priorities, and resources. Here are some methods to help you organize your time more effectively:

1. **Establish clear objectives**: To begin, list your immediate and long-term objectives. When and what do you aim to achieve? Having clear goals in mind makes it easier to prioritize your tasks and manage your time.
2. **Break down tasks**: Divide enormous goals into smaller, more manageable tasks or action stages. This makes them less intimidating and easier to manage. Set deadlines or goal dates for each task to hold yourself accountable.
3. **Estimate Time Requirements**: Determine how long each task will take to accomplish. Be realistic in your projections and leave some extra time for unanticipated delays or disruptions.
4. **Allocate Resources**: Think about the resources you'll need to perform each task, whether they're time, money, or other resources. Make sure you have everything you need before getting started, and plan accordingly.
5. **Identify Dependencies**: Determine whether any tasks rely on others and manage your schedule accordingly. For example, you may need to finish one activity before beginning another, or you may require feedback or support from others.
6. **Establish Milestones**: Divide your goals into smaller milestones or checkpoints. Celebrate your accomplishments as you reach each milestone, and use them as an incentive to keep going.
7. **Review and Adjust**: Regularly review your plans and make any necessary adjustments. It's acceptable when things don't always go according to plan. Be flexible and receptive to new circumstances.

By putting these effective planning strategies into practice, you can maximize your time and set yourself up for success.

Creating To-Do Lists

To-do lists are a simple yet effective way to organize your work and remain on track. Here are some suggestions for making efficient to-do lists:

1. **Keep It Simple**: Avoid overwhelming yourself with a big, convoluted to-do list. Keep things simple and focus on the most critical chores of the day or week.
2. **Priorities Tasks**: Arrange your tasks in order of priority or urgency. This ensures that you priorities the most important tasks and make progress towards your goals.
3 **Break jobs down**: Divide larger jobs into smaller, more manageable subtasks. This makes them less scary and easier to handle.
4. **Use Clear Language**: When documenting your tasks, use clear and simple language. Avoid obscure or confusing terminology that could cause confusion.
5. **Set deadlines or goal dates** for each task to keep yourself accountable and motivated. Set realistic timelines and allow for some flexibility when needed.
6. **Review and update regularly**: On a regular basis, review your to-do list and make any necessary updates. Add new tasks as they appear, and mark them off as they are completed. This keeps your list current and ensures that nothing slips through the cracks.
7. **Limit distractions**: Make sure the items on your to-do list are pertinent to your priorities and ambitions. Steer clear of unneeded chores and distractions that could lower your productivity.

Including to-do lists in your weekly or daily routine will help you stay focused, organized, and on track to achieve your goals.

Utilizing Time Blocking and Calendars

Calendars and time blocking are helpful tools for properly planning and managing your time. How to use them is as follows:

1. **Time Blocking**: Time blocking is the process of breaking your day into specified blocks of time for certain jobs or activities. This reduces multitasking and guarantees that you devote focused time to your most critical responsibilities. Begin by identifying the most critical chores for the day or week.

Schedule blocks of time for each task, leaving enough time for breaks or unexpected interruptions.

Stick to your schedule as much as possible and fight the urge to deviate from your time blocks.

2. **Calendar Management**: Utilize a calendar or scheduling tool to arrange your schedule and keep track of critical deadlines and appointments.

Input all of your projects, appointments, and deadlines into your calendar, including essential information like location, time, and any necessary preparation.

To stay on top of your commitments and make changes as needed, regularly review your calendar.

To help keep tasks or activities organized, consider color-coding or utilizing separate calendars for each category.

3. **Sync across Devices**: Make sure your calendar is easily available from all of your devices, including your computer, smartphone, and tablet. This allows you to view your itinerary from anywhere and keep organized while travelling.

By combining time blocks and calendars into your time management toolkit, you can better manage your schedule, priorities your responsibilities, and maximize your available time.

Overcoming Procrastination

Procrastination is the quiet thief of time. It depletes our productivity, disrupts our plans, and leaves us feeling stressed and disappointed. Despite our best intentions, we frequently fall for its enticing appeal. In this section, we'll look at the psychology of procrastination, proven tactics for overcoming it, and how to develop the discipline and motivation required to stay on track.

Understanding Procrastination

Procrastination is the practice of delaying or postponing chores or activities in order to prevent unpleasant emotions or discomfort. It's a widespread occurrence that affects people of all ages and backgrounds, and it can take many forms, from postponing crucial professional assignments to delaying domestic duties or personal aspirations.

Procrastination is typically motivated by a combination of fear, perfectionism, and low self-esteem. We delay because we are terrified of failure or rejection, because we are perfectionists who are concerned about not meeting our own high standards, or because we mistrust our talents and believe we are not good enough. Understanding the root causes of procrastination is the first step towards conquering it. Recognizing the patterns and thinking processes that contribute to our procrastination habits enables us to begin developing methods to overcome them and regain control of our time.

Proven Strategies to Beat Procrastination

While conquering procrastination is not a simple task, there are some tried-and-true tactics that can help. To overcome procrastination and increase productivity, consider 1.**Breaking down work** into manageable chunks. Break down enormous activities into smaller, more manageable steps and focus on completing one at a time. This makes the task seem more manageable and less frightening.

2. **Establish clear goals**: Having clear, defined goals provides you with something tangible to work towards and keeps you motivated. Set short- and long-term goals and divide them into actionable stages. This gives you a road map for your progress and helps you stay focused on what has to be done.
3. **Use the Pomodoro Technique**: The Pomodoro Technique is a time management strategy that entails working in short bursts of focused effort, usually lasting 25 minutes, followed by a short break. This helps to divide activities into small portions and prevent fatigue. Set a timer for 25 minutes and work on a task with complete attention, then take a brief rest before beginning the next Pomodoro.
4. **Establish Accountability**: Share your goals and deadlines with a friend, family member, or colleague. Having someone hold you accountable might help you stay motivated and on task. To help you stay focused on your goals, consider joining a support group or working with an accountability partner.
5. **Practice self-compassion**: When dealing with procrastination, be compassionate to yourself. Recognize that procrastination is a normal human experience and does not define your worth as a person. Instead of berating yourself for procrastination, practice self-compassion and focus on making good efforts to overcome it.
6. **Eliminate Distractions**: Identify and remove any potential distractions that may be contributing to your procrastination. This could mean turning off your phone's notifications, blocking distracting websites, or finding a quiet, clutter-free office where you can concentrate without interruptions.
7. **Reward Yourself**: Recognize yourself for making progress towards your objectives, no matter how modest. Celebrate your accomplishments and milestones along the way, whether with a modest reward, a break, or an enjoyable activity. This reinforces positive behaviors and keeps you motivated to continue making improvements.

Cultivating Discipline and Motivation

Discipline and motivation are crucial traits for overcoming procrastination and mastering time management. Here are some suggestions for developing these qualities:
1. **Set intentions**. Begin each day with a clear aim for what you hope to accomplish. Visualize yourself finishing your duties and reaching your goals, and then commit to taking action towards them.
2. **Establish a pattern**: Having a daily pattern will help you build structure and discipline in your life. Set out a specific time each day for work, exercise, self-care, and relaxation, and stick to it as much as possible.

3. **Develop Self-Discipline**: Self-discipline is the capacity to control your impulses and remain focused on your goals in the face of distractions or temptations. Set limits, say no to distractions, and keep your promises.

4. **Discover Your Why**: Determine your underlying motives and reasons for wanting to overcome procrastination and improve your time management skills. Whether it's attaining a personal goal, moving up in your job, or enhancing your quality of life, having a strong reason can help you stay motivated during difficult times.

5. **Celebrate Progress**: Recognize your progress and accomplishments along the way. Recognize minor victories and milestones, and use them as fuel to keep you motivated and progressing.

6. **Maintain Flexibility**: While discipline is essential, it is also crucial to maintain flexibility and adaptability. Life is unforeseeable, and not everything goes as planned. Be open to changing your goals and plans as needed, and don't be too hard on yourself if things don't go as planned.

Understanding procrastination's psychology, employing tried-and-true strategies, and cultivating discipline and motivation will help you overcome it and take control of your schedule.

Optimizing Productivity

Productivity is the key to reaching your goals and making the best use of your time. By increasing your productivity, you can complete more tasks in less time, reduce stress, and improve your overall effectiveness. In this section, we'll look at numerous ideas and techniques for increasing your productivity and getting more done.

Find your peak productivity hours
Everyone has certain moments of the day when they feel the most alert, focused, and energized. These are your peak productivity hours, and identifying them will allow you to optimize your calendar for optimal efficiency. Here's how to determine your peak production hours:
1. **Monitor your energy levels**: Pay attention to your energy levels throughout the day, noting when you feel the most awake and alert. This can differ from person to person, so it's critical to tune into your own body and listen to its messages.
2. **Experiment with Different Times**: Try working at different times of the day. Some people are early birds and work best in the morning, while others are night owls and prefer to work later in the day. Determine what works best for you, and schedule your most critical chores during your peak production hours.
3. Pay attention to trends: Look for any persistent trends in your energy levels. For example, you may get a burst of energy after exercising or feel more concentrated after eating. Use these patterns to your advantage, and plan your duties accordingly.
4. **Minimize Distractions**: During your peak productivity hours, try to avoid distractions and interruptions. This could include shutting off notifications on your phone, closing unneeded tabs on your computer, or finding a quiet office where you can concentrate without distractions.
5. **Take Breaks**: Even during high productivity hours, it's critical to take regular breaks to rest and recharge. Schedule small pauses every hour or so to stretch, hydrate, and allow your brain to relax before getting back to work.
By identifying your peak production hours and arranging your most critical tasks accordingly, you can maximize your energy and accomplish more in less time.

Implementing focus and concentration techniques
Maintaining attention and concentration is vital for increasing productivity and completing tasks. Here are some ways that will help you stay focused and avoid distractions.
1. **Establish clear goals**: Setting clear, detailed goals provides you with a sense of purpose and direction, making it simpler to stay focused on your duties. Break down your goals into smaller, more practical actions and priorities them according to priority and urgency.
2. **Use Time Blocking**: Time blocking entails allocating specified blocks of time for various tasks or activities. This reduces distractions and allows you to concentrate on a single task at a time without interruption.
3. **Practice mindfulness**: Techniques like meditation and deep breathing exercises can help you focus and concentrate more effectively. Take a few minutes each day to practice mindfulness and cleanse your thoughts of distractions before beginning work.
4. **Limit Multitasking**: Contrary to common opinion, multitasking is not a productive approach to getting things done. Instead of attempting to juggle numerous activities at once, concentrate on one at a time and give it your undivided attention before proceeding to the next.
5. **Use the Pomodoro Technique**: The Pomodoro Technique is a time management technique that entails working in short bursts of focused effort, usually lasting 25 minutes, followed by a short break. This prevents burnout and allows you to stay focused and concentrated for extended periods of time.
6. **Minimize Distractions**: Identify and eliminate any potential distractions that could interfere with your concentration, such as noise, clutter, or social media. Use technologies like internet blockers or noise-cancelling headphones to create a distraction-free work environment.
Implementing these focus and concentration skills will help you increase your productivity and make the most of your time.

Tools and apps for productivity enhancement
In today's digital age, there are several tools and apps available to help you boost productivity and optimize your workflows. Here are some popular alternatives to consider:
1. **Task Management Apps**: Apps like Todoist, Trello, and Asana may help you organize tasks, set deadlines, and measure your progress. These applications are excellent for organizing your to-do lists and ensuring that nothing goes between the gaps.

2. **Note-Taking Apps**: Apps like Ever note and Microsoft OneNote enable you to record ideas, write down notes, and organize your thoughts in a single area. These apps are ideal for managing crucial information and remaining organized.
3. **Time Tracking Apps**: Apps like Toggle or Rescue Time help you measure how you spend your time and discover areas for improvement. These programmed can provide significant insights into your productivity habits, allowing you to make better decisions about how to spend your time.
4. **Focus Apps**: Focus apps, such as Forest or Focus @Will, help you stay focused and prevent distractions by restricting access to distracting websites or playing background music that improves concentration. These apps are excellent for creating a distraction-free workplace and increasing productivity.
5. **Calendar Apps**: Calendar apps, such as Google Calendar or Apple Calendar, allow you to schedule projects, appointments, and deadlines while staying organized. These applications sync across all of your devices, so you can easily view your schedule no matter where you are.
6. **Automation technologies**: Automation solutions like Zippier and IFTTT can help you automate monotonous tasks and increase your productivity. These applications will allow you to save time and effort.

Managing Distractions

Distractions are the enemy of productivity, drawing our attention away from critical work and diverting our focus. In today's fast-paced environment, where we are constantly assaulted with notifications, emails, and other disruptions, minimizing distractions is critical for maximizing our time and completing our objectives. In this section, we'll look at frequent distractions, ways to reduce them, and how to build an optimal work environment for productivity.

Identifying common distractions
Distractions can take many different forms, from external stimuli like noise and interruptions to internal reasons like procrastination and multitasking. Here are a few common distractions to be wary of:
1. **Technology**: Smartphones, social media, and email are among the most common sources of distraction in today's digital world. Notifications, notifications, and constant connectivity can distract us from our work and break our concentration.
2. **Noise**: Whether it's chatting from coworkers, construction outside your office, or the hum of traffic, disturbances may be a huge distraction at work. It can interfere with our ability to concentrate on tasks.
3. **Interruptions**: Coworkers, phone calls, and unexpected guests can all break our workflow and impede our mental process. Even small interruptions can take time to recover and resume normal operations.
4. **Multitasking**: Contrary to popular belief, multitasking is not a productive way to work. Switching between tasks demands mental effort, which can lead to lower productivity and more errors.
5. **Procrastination**: Procrastination is the act of delaying or postponing duties, typically to avoid discomfort or unpleasant feelings. It can be a huge source of distraction, preventing us from moving forward with our goals.
6. **Clutter**: A cluttered workstation can be visually distracting, making it harder to concentrate on work. Decluttering and organizing your workstation can help create a more productive environment.

Techniques for Minimizing Distractions
While it is hard to completely remove distractions, you can use various ways to reduce their impact and stay focused on your work:
1. **Establish Boundaries**: To minimize distractions, set clear boundaries around your time and space. Inform coworkers when you need undisturbed time to focus, and establish specific hours for reading emails or responding to messages.
2. **Use Do Not Disturb option**: Use your phone or computer's "Do Not Disturb" feature to silence messages and reduce disruptions during focused work sessions.
3. **Designate a Distraction-Free Zone**: Set aside a certain section of your office for uninterrupted concentration. This might be a quiet nook in your office or a separate workspace at home.
4. **Batch Tasks**: Combine related tasks and complete them in batches to reduce the mental work necessary to transition between tasks. Instead of checking email or returning phone calls at random intervals throughout the day, set aside defined periods for these tasks.
5. **Use time blocking**: Set aside specific blocks of time in your schedule for focused work without distractions. Use this time to complete your most important tasks while minimizing distractions by turning off notifications and closing unneeded tabs or windows.
6. **Use Focus** Apps: Several apps are available to help you stay focused and avoid distractions by preventing access to distracting websites or apps. Examples include freedom, cold turkey, and staying focused.
7. **Take pauses**: Schedule regular pauses throughout the day to rest and recover. Taking breaks from your work can help you avoid burnout and boost your overall productivity.

Creating an optimal work environment
Creating an appropriate working environment is critical for reducing distractions and increasing productivity. Here are some suggestions for making a workstation conducive to focus and concentration:
1. **Declutter:** Remove clutter from your desk to create a clean, organized environment. Keep only the essentials close at hand, and keep anything you don't use on a regular basis out of sight.
2. **Control the Noise**: Reduce noise distractions by using noise-cancelling headphones, listening to white noise or relaxing music, or moving to a quieter environment if possible.

3. **Set up ergonomically**: Arrange your workspace to maximize comfort and efficiency. To reduce eye strain, use an adjustable chair, set your display at eye level, and provide adequate illumination.

4. **Personalize Your Space**: Decorate your workstation with items that inspire and motivate you, such as photographs, plants, or artwork. Surrounding oneself with things you enjoy can help create a happy and welcoming environment.

5. **Establish Rituals**: Make customs or routines to alert your brain that it is time to concentrate and work. This may entail making a cup of coffee, listening to a specific playlist, or performing a little mindfulness exercise before beginning your chores.

6. **Establish Clear Boundaries**: Set boundaries with coworkers, family members, or roommates to reduce disruptions during focused work time. Communicate your wants and expectations clearly, so that others will respect your time and space.

By following these tactics and creating an ideal work environment, you may reduce distractions while increasing productivity, allowing you to make the most of your time and achieve your objectives.

Delegating and Outsourcing

Delegating duties and outsourcing non-essential operations are critical tactics for time management. You can maximize your productivity and make the best use of your time by dispersing your workload and focusing on high-priority projects. In this section, we'll look at the art of delegation, effective delegation tactics, and the advantages of outsourcing non-essential jobs.

Knowing when to delegate
knowing when to delegate is critical to good time management. Here are several signs that it could be time to subcontract a task:
1. **Time constraints**: If you feel overwhelmed by tasks and unable to keep up with your job, it may be time to outsource some responsibility to others.
2. **Skills Gap**: If a task demands skills or experience that you do not have, it may be more efficient to delegate it to someone who is more suited to the work.
3. **Low Priority**: Tasks that are low priority or outside of your area of expertise can frequently be delegated in order to free up time for more critical operations.
4. **Opportunity expense**: Consider the cost of carrying out a task yourself rather than delegating it to someone else. Delegating the task may be worthwhile if it allows you to devote more time to higher-value activities.
5. **Development Opportunities**: Delegating work can help team members grow by allowing them to take on new responsibilities and broaden their abilities.
Recognizing when to delegate responsibilities allows you to devote more time and energy to activities that are in line with your goals and priorities.

Effective delegation strategies
Effective delegation necessitates careful preparation and communication to ensure that tasks are properly accomplished. Here are some ways to successfully distribute tasks:
1. **Clearly define tasks**: Clearly outline the task you're assigning, including objectives, expectations, and any applicable dates or standards. Give the delegate specific instructions and resources to help them understand what they need to do.

2. **Assign responsibility appropriately**: Delegate duties that are appropriate for the person's skills and abilities. When distributing responsibilities, take into account things including experience, competence, and workload.
3. **Communicate expectations**: Clearly describe your task expectations, including intended outcomes, dates, and any unique requirements or limits. Encourage open communication and offer help when required.
4. **Provide Resources and Support**: Make sure the person you're delegating to have access to the resources, tools, and information will need to accomplish the assignment successfully. To ensure their success, provide direction, training, and support as needed.
5. **Establish check-in points**: Create check-in points or milestones to track progress and provide feedback along the way. This allows you to course-correct as needed and keeps the task on track.
6. **Trust and Empower**: Trust the person you're delegating to, and give them the authority to make decisions and take ownership of the assignment. Avoid micromanagement and give them the freedom to finish the assignment in their own way.
7. **Acknowledge and Appreciate**: Regardless of the outcome, recognize and appreciate the efforts of the person you're delegating to. Recognize their contributions and provide constructive feedback to assist their growth and development.

By implementing these effective delegation tactics, you may enable others to take on chores and responsibilities, freeing up your time to focus on more valuable activities.

Outsourcing non-essential tasks

Outsourcing non-essential jobs is yet another effective approach to increasing productivity and efficiency. Delegating jobs to external vendors or contractors allows you to benefit from specialized skills while focusing on key business activities.

The following are some common non-essential duties that can be outsourced:
1. **Administrative Tasks**: Data entry, bookkeeping, scheduling, and email management are frequently outsourced to virtual assistants or administrative services.
2. **Design and Creative Work**: Graphic design, web design, and content development can all be outsourced to freelancers or creative companies.
3. **Technical Support**: IT support, software development, and website maintenance can all be delegated to specialized technical service providers.

4. **Marketing and Advertising**: Marketing and advertising responsibilities, such as social media management, advertising campaigns, and SEO optimization, can be delegated to marketing firms or freelancers.
5. **Customer Service**: Customer service responsibilities, including answering questions, addressing complaints, and processing purchases, can be delegated to contact centers or customer service agencies.
6. **Event Planning**: Tasks like venue selection, catering, and logistics coordination can be delegated to event planning businesses or independent event planners.

When outsourcing non-essential jobs, it is critical to thoroughly assess potential vendors or contractors, clarify expectations and needs, and establish effective communication channels. External knowledge can help you optimize your operations, cut expenses, and focus on activities that promote development and innovation.

Strategies for Time Recovery

Time is an invaluable resource, but it is also finite. Despite our best attempts to manage it properly, unexpected circumstances, disruptions, or crises might knock our plans off track. In this section, we will look at tactics for recovering lost time, dealing with interruptions and emergencies, and managing time during a crisis.

Handling Interruptions and Emergency

Interruptions and emergencies are unavoidable in both personal and professional settings. Disruptions, such as a phone call from a customer, a last-minute project request, or a sudden domestic emergency, can derail our plans and throw our schedules off. Here are some ways for managing interruptions and emergencies effectively:

1. **Stay Calm**: When confronted with an interruption or emergency, it is critical to remain calm and composed. Take a deep breath, examine the situation calmly, and determine your next moves.
2. **Determine Urgency**: Determine the urgency of the disruption or emergency and priorities your action. Is it something that requires immediate attention, or can it wait until you've completed your current task?
3. **Set boundaries**: Set boundaries for your time and availability to reduce disruptions. Inform colleagues, clients, or family members when you are accessible and when you require undisturbed time to focus.
4. **Delegate if Possible**: If the interruption or emergency requires work to be delegated to others, don't hesitate to do so. Delegating chores can help you free up time and focus on more important concerns.
5. **Communicate Effectively**: Be clear about your availability and any scheduling modifications caused by the disruption or emergency. Keep stakeholders aware of your work and provide updates when necessary.
6. **Reassess Priorities**: In light of the disruption or emergency, reassess your priorities and change your schedule accordingly.

Be adaptable and open to change conditions while remaining focused on your goals.

7. **Prepare for Contingencies**: Prepare for unexpected interruptions or emergencies and have a plan in place to handle them. This could involve scheduling buffer time or having backup resources accessible if necessary.

By applying these tactics, you can reduce the impact of interruptions and emergencies on your schedule while remaining focused on your priorities.

Time Management During Crisis Situations

Crisis circumstances, whether personal or professional, can disrupt our lives and put our schedules off track. During times of crisis, it's critical to priorities self-care, retain perspective, and concentrate on what's under your control. Here are some suggestions for managing time during crisis situations:

1. **Priorities Self-Care**: During a crisis, it is critical to prioritize one's own well-being. Get enough sleep, eat healthily, and participate in activities that reduce stress and encourage relaxation.

2. **Focus on the Essentials**: During a crisis, prioritize key tasks and duties that must be completed promptly. Let go of non-essential activities and obligations to free up time and energy for what is genuinely important.

3. **Set realistic expectations**: Be realistic about what you can accomplish during a crisis, and set achievable goals and expectations for yourself. Don't put too much pressure on yourself to be as productive as you normally are.

4. **Seek Support**: During a crisis, reach out to friends, family, or colleagues for help. Don't be scared to seek for help or outsource responsibilities to others when necessary. Surround yourself with a supportive group of people who can offer help and advice.

5. **Maintain Flexibility**: During a crisis, your approach to time management should be fluid and responsive. Things may not go as planned, and that's okay. Focus on remaining resilient and devising inventive solutions to problems as they emerge.

6. **Practice Mindfulness**: Incorporate mindfulness techniques into your daily routine, such as meditation, deep breathing exercises, or journaling, to assist manage stress and keep perspective during a crisis. Mindfulness can help you remain grounded and focused in the present moment.

7. **Priorities**: Prioritize what you can control during a crisis. Instead of fretting about things beyond your control, focus on taking positive action in areas where you can make a difference.

Techniques for Reclaiming Lost Time
When unexpected disruptions or emergencies occur, it is easy to become frustrated or overwhelmed. However, it is crucial to note that wasted time may frequently be recovered with the appropriate strategy. Here are several methods for restoring lost time:
1. **Priorities Tasks**: Determine which tasks were interrupted or postponed due to the emergency and priorities them according to priority and urgency. To reduce the impact of missed time, priorities completing the most vital activities.
2. **Reallocate Resources**: Use resources such as time, people, or budget to complete projects that were postponed or put on hold during the emergency. Be strategic in your resource deployment to ensure that you make the most of what you have.
3. **Adjust Deadlines**: If necessary, revise deadlines or expectations for work affected by the emergency. Communicate with stakeholders to renegotiate timelines and establish reasonable expectations for work completion times.
4. **Implement Time Recovery Techniques**: Use time recovery techniques like time blocking, the Pomodoro Technique, or batching comparable work to increase productivity and make up for lost time.
5. **Learn from Your Experience**: Take some time to reflect on the emergency and identify any lessons learned or opportunities for improvement. Use the experience to build your resilience and develop techniques for dealing with similar situations in the future.
6. **Practice Forgiveness**: When faced with a crisis, be kind to yourself and practice self-compassion. Recognize that it is normal to face setbacks and hardships, and forgive yourself for any perceived flaws or missteps.
7. **Maintain a good Outlook**: Instead of obsessing on lost time, keep a good attitude and focus on the progress you've accomplished. Celebrate minor triumphs and milestones along the road to keep yourself motivated and on track.
Implementing these tactics allows you to efficiently manage interruptions, emergencies, and crisis situations while recuperating lost time and remaining focused on your goals.

Maintaining Work-Life Balance

Work-life balance is a careful mix of professional responsibilities and personal well-being. In today's fast-paced world, where technology blurs the distinction between work and personal life, striking and keeping this balance is more difficult than ever. In this section, we'll look at the importance of work-life balance, boundary-setting procedures, and self-care and relaxation approaches to improve general well-being.

The importance of work-life balance

Work-life balance is critical to general health and happiness. Here are some reasons why developing and maintaining a work-life balance is critical:

1. **Health and Well-Being**: A balanced lifestyle benefits both physical and mental health. Chronic stress from overworking or disregarding personal needs can result in burnout, anxiety, and other health problems.
2. **Increased Productivity**: Taking time to relax and recharge allows you to return to work feeling renewed and invigorated, resulting in higher productivity and efficiency.
3. **Improved Relationships**: Spending quality time with loved ones deepens bonds and fosters a sense of connection and identity.
4. **Personal Fulfilment**: Pursuing interests and hobbies outside of work provides a sense of fulfilment and purpose that extends beyond professional achievements.
5. **Reduced Burnout**: Keeping a healthy work-life balance helps avoid burnout and boosts resilience in the face of adversity.
6. **Increased Creativity and Innovation**: Taking time away from work helps your mind wander and find connections, resulting in more creativity and innovation.
7. **Improved Quality of Life**: Finally, work-life balance leads to a higher quality of life, helping you to achieve both professional success and personal fulfilment.

Setting Boundaries

Setting boundaries is critical for achieving work-life balance and preventing work from interfering with personal time. Here are several techniques to set boundaries:

1. **Establish clear work hours**: Set specific work hours and adhere to them as much as possible. Communicate your availability with coworkers, clients, and supervisors to manage expectations and reduce the after-hours workload.
2. **Schedule Personal Time**: Set aside time for personal pursuits, hobbies, and leisure. Treat this time as precious and prioritize it like you would any other business commitment. 3. **Set boundaries for digital use** to keep work-related emails, calls, and messages from interfering with personal time. Consider setting limits, such as shutting off notifications or keeping work electronics in a separate room during your personal time.

4. **Say no when necessary**: Learn to say no to requests and obligations that do not match your priorities or values. Setting boundaries for your time and energy is critical to maintaining a work-life balance.
5. **Delegate chores**: When possible, delegate chores and obligations to others in order to reduce your workload and make more time for personal interests. Trust your coworkers and allow them to take on additional responsibility as needed.
6. **Use time-blocking techniques**: schedule certain blocks of time for work, personal pursuits, and rest. This ensures that you allocate time for all aspects of your life while avoiding over commitment.
7. **Communicate Openly**: Be upfront with colleagues, superiors, and loved ones about your boundaries and requirements. To minimize misunderstandings and resentment, make it clear what you can and cannot accommodate.

Practice self-care and relaxation techniques

Self-care and relaxation strategies are critical for replenishing your batteries and preserving general health. Here are some ways to practice self-care and relaxation:
1. **Exercise regularly**: Regular physical activity can help reduce stress, enhance mood, and boost energy levels. Find activities that you enjoy, whether it's going for a stroll, doing yoga, or playing sports.
2. **Prioritize:** Sleep: Make sleep a priority by sticking to a regular sleep schedule and developing a calming nighttime routine. Aim for seven to nine hours of quality sleep per night to improve your overall health and well-being.
3. **Practice mindfulness**: Make meditation, deep breathing exercises, and journaling part of your daily routine. Mindfulness reduces stress, improves self-awareness, and promotes relaxation.
4. **Unplug frequently**: Take breaks from technology and screens to refresh your mind and reconnect with the present moment. Spend time in nature, participate in creative pursuits, or simply enjoy quiet moments alone.
5. **Nurture ties**: Develop meaningful ties with your friends, family, and loved ones. Make time for regular social encounters and value quality time spent together.
6. **Indulge in Hobbies**: Find activities and interests that bring you joy and fulfilment. Hobbies outside of work, such as gardening, cooking, painting, or playing music, nurture the soul and promote creativity.

7. **Set aside time for leisure and self-care activities**: Take a relaxing bubble bath, read a good book, or simply do nothing.

Prioritizing self-care and relaxation allows you to recharge your batteries, reduce stress, and improve general well-being, resulting in a more balanced and meaningful existence.

CONCLUSION

Mastering the Clock

Time is the most precious resource we have. It's finite, irreplaceable, and constantly ticking away, regardless of how we choose to spend it. In the fast-paced world we live in, mastering time management is essential for achieving our goals, fulfilling our responsibilities, and living a balanced and fulfilling life.

Throughout this comprehensive guide, we've explored various strategies, techniques, and principles for mastering the clock and maximizing our time. From setting clear goals and priorities to overcoming procrastination, managing distractions, and practicing self-care, each aspect of time management plays a vital role in our overall productivity and well-being.

Reflecting on the Journey

Our journey began by understanding the importance of time management and recognizing the need to take control of our schedules and priorities. We explored the fundamental principles of time management, including goal setting, prioritization, planning, and delegation, laying the foundation for effective time management practices.

We delved into self-awareness techniques to assess our current time usage, identify time wasters, and analyze our daily routines for opportunities to optimize productivity. By understanding our strengths, weaknesses, and habits, we gained valuable insights into where we can make improvements and take proactive steps to manage our time more effectively.

Setting clear goals and priorities emerged as a cornerstone of effective time management. By defining our objectives, breaking them down into actionable steps, and aligning our daily activities with our long-term aspirations, we created a roadmap for success and focused our efforts on what truly matters.

We explored proven techniques for planning and scheduling, including creating to-do lists, utilizing time blocking, and harnessing the power of calendars and productivity tools. These strategies empowered us to take control of our time, manage competing priorities, and ensure that our days are structured for maximum efficiency and effectiveness.

Overcoming procrastination emerged as a common challenge in our journey towards mastering the clock. By understanding the underlying causes of procrastination and implementing proven strategies to beat it, we learned to cultivate discipline, motivation, and focus, enabling us to tackle tasks with confidence and purpose.

Optimizing productivity became a key focus as we explored techniques for finding our peak productivity hours, implementing focus and concentration strategies, and leveraging tools and apps to enhance efficiency. By harnessing our natural rhythms and utilizing productivity-enhancing tools, we unlocked new levels of productivity and accomplished more in less time.

Managing distractions emerged as a critical skill in our quest for effective time management. By identifying common distractions, minimizing interruptions, and creating optimal work environments, we cultivated focus, concentration, and resilience in the face of distractions, allowing us to stay on track and maintain productivity.

In times of crisis and upheaval, we learned valuable strategies for time recovery, handling interruptions and emergencies, and regaining lost time. By staying calm, flexible, and focused on our priorities, we navigated challenges with grace and resilience, emerging stronger and more resilient than before.

Maintaining a work-life balance became our ultimate goal on our journey, we achieved harmony between our professional responsibilities and personal well-being by recognizing the need for work-life balance, setting boundaries, and applying self-care and relaxation routines, which resulted in more happiness, contentment, and success in all parts of our lives.

Looking Forward

As we conclude our journey of mastering the clock, let us carry forward the lessons learned and principles embraced into our daily lives. Let us continue to prioritize our time, set clear goals and priorities, and practice self-awareness and discipline in managing our schedules and commitments.

Let us remain vigilant against the pitfalls of procrastination, distraction, and overwhelm, and cultivate resilience, focus, and productivity in the face of challenges. Let us embrace change, adapt to new circumstances, and approach time management with creativity, flexibility, and a growth mindset.

Above all, let us remember that time is not a resource to be hoarded or squandered but a gift to be cherished and invested wisely. By mastering the clock and making the most of our time, we can unlock our full potential, achieve our dreams, and create a life of purpose, passion, and fulfillment.

Benjamin Franklin once said, "Do you love life? Then don't waste time, because that's what life is built of." Let us hear these words and set out to manage the clock with diligence, effort, and a firm resolve to making every moment matter.

Time is yours to Master

The journey to mastering the clock is a lifelong endeavor, not a destination. It requires dedication, discipline, and a willingness to continually learn and grow. As you go out on your own route to perfect time management, remember that you have the potential to create your own future. The clock is running out, and it's time to act. So, accept the challenge, take the opportunity, and set out on the path to master the clock with courage, conviction, and a sense of purpose. You have control over your time. Make it count.

www.ingramcontent.com/pod-product-compliance
Lightning Source LLC
Chambersburg PA
CBHW050251230526
45470CB00005B/2211